TEENAGERS CLOSER TO GOD

Derek F. Rochford

GN00983555

CTS Publications

First published 1993 by the
Incorporated Catholic Truth Society
38–40 Eccleston Square
London SW1V 1PD

© *1993 The Incorporated Catholic Truth Society*

ISBN 0 865183 882 0

TEENAGERS CLOSER TO GOD

Introduction:

You don't have to be a good Catholic to find this booklet useful. In fact, you don't have to be a Catholic at all. Most young people feel unhappy about the evils in the world, and deep down inside themselves often suspect that much of the effort put into relieving misery by all sorts of organizations who promote their "good causes" is simply scratching at the surface and dealing with symptoms.

Somehow, they feel that there are deeper needs which are not being addressed, in fact a deeper longing within their own selves which is not satisfied by any form of escape – whether they find an outlet for their generosity and sadness in helping the many good causes, or try to distract themselves with earthly relationships and ambitions (however praiseworthy), or turn to the attractions of alcohol or drugs. Always that longing is there, and it means that God is calling them. He has made each of us by his own special choice in preference to any other person that he might have made, and he did so because he loves us and longs for a return of that love.

This booklet will help you to reach out to the cause of this longing, which of course is God himself. For the moment, please be willing to take my word for it that nothing and nobody else can ever satisfy you completely.

Go slowly through this booklet. The ideas are numbered separately to show some of the places where you will find it helpful to stop and think about what you have been reading. You may sometimes come across a point which strikes you in the middle of a section: then stop and think. Above all, never set yourself a fixed amount to be read at one sitting. The booklet is meant to help stimulate your thoughts about yourself and Jesus, and to help you pass from thinking about him to prayer, which after all is simply raising your mind and heart to him with all the love you can. Try not to set yourself too close a time-limit on these occasions, for prayer is not one-sided; be silent sometimes and give Jesus a chance to answer with his grace bringing ideas to your mind if he wishes to do so.

This is not a theological treatise, nor is it meant to tell you all you may want to know about God and yourself. If it succeeds in setting you on the path to knowing God better and trying sincerely to love him, it will have been valuable to you. There will be all sorts of difficulties along the way, partly because we find it hard to aim at high ideals and stick at them, and partly because Satan will try in all sorts of ways to hold you back. Don't be discouraged. If you can, talk over difficulties as they arise, with a close friend (perhaps a priest if you know one and feel you can confide in him). To Jesus, you are worth his suffering and dying for you, and nothing else is as important as that.

TEENAGERS CLOSER TO GOD

1 A person is more or less holy to the extent that they are more or less like Jesus, who is the Son of God, of one being with him, and totally united with him in mind and will, the sinless one, both human and divine.

2 God has no grandchildren: we have our share in his divine life directly from him at our Baptism, so that the Faith as you were taught it by your parents you must make your own because you are God's child directly; you do not have your share in God's life through your parents as you do your natural life. Your parents passed on the Faith to you because they wanted to make sure that you received from them the truth (for your eternal salvation). So this Faith must take root in you, partly for your own self, but also because *your* children will have the right to receive it from *you*, just as you had the right to receive it from your parents. "Partly for your own self" because it gives you the framework for developing your own relationship with God. Why is this needed and how does it come about?

3 Everyone has deepset questions: Who and what am I? Why am I here, what am I for? One day I shall die, and what then? (There are other questions too, like the problems of evil and suffering, but they must come later). Because we humans have clouded minds and weak wills (the result of original sin), we can be corrupted by greed, fear and prejudice, so that many will try to turn their backs on these questions. But they won't go away.

4 As well as these questions, we have deepset self-regarding instincts, notably self-respect, which in extremes shows as self-preservation. Because of our fallen nature, we long to be well thought of and to be wanted, we need to be loved. Provided that we don't allow our self-respect to grow out of control and become pride, it can help us to seek God with the aid of his grace, and we can find him through our deepest desires and longings (think of your powers of mind, will, memory, imagination and the good hopes and ideals that these can put before you – but if you become proud, through these powers you will seek to raise yourself regardless of others, who will suffer as a result).

Only God can satisfy your deepest longings, and he reaches out to draw you to himself. He loves you because he made you, and therefore you are his child, unique, different from all others as you instinctively feel yourself to be. When your parents decided to have you, God made you, creating your soul from nothing by the direct act of his will, and implanting it in you at the moment of your conception. Thus he gave you your individual selfness, your special differentness from all others. This is the spiritual part of you, and it can never die.

5 Your soul is not the same as your brain – a corpse has a brain but it is an empty house. While your body is alive, your soul works through your brain, and its chief powers are your mind and your will. You use your mind directed by your will to acquire knowledge, to find things out. Your mind is designed for this purpose and desires to do it – hence you ask questions. Your mind has two subsidiary powers, your memory for storing what you know, and your imagination to help you to reason ahead. You use your will for choosing; it is your power of accepting and rejecting (loving and hating, liking and disliking).

Your will is blind, in the sense that it chooses on the basis of what your mind presents to it. You always decide on the basis of what your mind (you) considers to be good and therefore desirable. Even if you choose what you know to be wrong, you still choose it because you see some aspect in it that makes it desirable and good. This goes against your conscience, which is your mind telling you, often under God's grace (see 10 and 11 below) that your choice is wrong, and we call such a choice sinful: sin is a deliberate decision of the will to take a line which we know to be opposed to our love of God in what we think, say, do or leave undone.

6 Where do your emotions fit in? They are your feelings, and they influence the way you react to things that influence you (people and how they behave towards you, things and events and how they affect you). How you feel about things (that is, how you react to them) is partly a matter of temperament, your makeup. This is partly inherited and partly acquired by the way you are treated, especially early in life. Your feelings cannot affect your existing knowledge, though they can affect the

future working of your mind. They will be stored in your memory, and may be triggered by powerful events. They can therefore affect your use of your will, and they will certainly influence your decisions if you feel strongly about something or somebody. Very strong emotions of fear, grief or rage can affect our decisions to such an extent that we may sometimes cease to be fully capable of free will, so that we are no longer fully responsible for our actions.

7 When you are faced with a decision to be made, it is important first to consider what is God's will for you, and to ask his guidance. Even after this you may still need advice, and at such a time it is good to have somebody you can turn to (perhaps family, a close friend, maybe a priest – whoever you think will help you best in the circumstances), because God may choose to show you his will in this way.

8 Although your mind and your will are your most important powers, your feelings still have their necessary place, for they often play a large part in the longings we experience (especially in the late teens). The feelings of insecurity (often hidden behind a macho front), of longing to be wanted, to be needed, to be loved in a different way from the love of our parents – these are all of them important. They change as we grow older, but the needs which give rise to the feelings will always be there. Why?

9 Here we come back to God again, and to the relationship between you and him. When you reach the teens you may reach a point when you begin to ask questions about the Catholic Faith in order to understand it more fully, and that is the time to ensure that it is deeply rooted in you. But this needs more help than just the answering of your questions. It needs God to help too, and you need his grace if you are to see that you need him.

10 He gives you that help (we call it grace), all the more if you respond to it by trying to reach out to him. That's praying: trying to be with him in your mind (whether you use words or not) and trying to love him in your will. Here your feelings will help, because that is where you experience your sense of

aloneness (I mean something deeper and sadder than loneliness), of not having something to satisfy the longings that are deepest within you and perhaps not yet fully recognized for what they are. He knows your feelings and how much you need him, for you are his child, and he will always answer.

What you need is his peace, and this can only come to you if you love him, trust him and obey him. Then you will know his love and his peace. Jesus Christ died to gain eternal life for you, and this consists of God's supernatural life in your soul, God's love living within you. He helps you to respond by loving him for his own sake; the more you respond, the closer and deeper your union with him will become. This brings you his peace, which is a peace that the world cannot give you.

11 How does he respond? By guiding your mind and will day by day (if you ask him). This is where conscience comes in: it is not itself God's voice; it is your mind in its present state of knowledge (and therefore fallible) pointing out to you, when you are faced with a choice, that to choose one way would be right, and the other way would be wrong, or perhaps at least a morally less good choice. If you allow him to guide you, you will become more sensitive to his promptings and he will draw you closer to himself. But remember that this sort of spiritual growth needs also the help of prayer – you need to respond to his guidance.

12 It will be useful to have a few clear ideas of the different starting-points of prayer. Basically prayer is of four kinds, though it can contain more than one at a time. These are adoring God (this includes praise and especially love), thanking him, being sorry for sin (ours and those of others), and asking him for what we need (for ourselves and others).

13 Before developing those ideas, it will help to say a little about the bases on which your spiritual life rests. Earlier we mentioned faith, or rather "the Faith". That meant our set of Catholic beliefs and practices, but now we need to think of faith as the gift of the Holy Spirit which is the essential bedrock of your relationship with God. In this sense it is often linked with hope and charity. Faith is believing everything that God has told us, hope is trusting that he will give us eternal joy with

him, and all the grace we need to reach it, charity is loving him for his own dear sake and loving others because he loves them. We cannot acquire the ability to do these things without his help.

(Note that it is the duty of his Church to safeguard our set of Catholic beliefs for us by its interpretation of the Scriptures and tradition under his guidance).

14 An important digression: it's all very well to talk about believing what God tells us, but what do I say to those who are not sure that there is a God at all? It would be no use saying that we believe in God because the Bible tells us to and the Bible is the word of God – that's arguing in a circle. No – it is possible to come to know something of God by reason unaided by faith, but this will only come about if somebody wants it to – it is quite possible for people to shut their minds to the possibility, because they are afraid that believing in God will bring obligations with it.

There are several well-known approaches, especially the need for an uncaused cause, and the fact that everything that exists has had to obtain its existence from a being which itself must always have existed. Or the one you may find most appealing is the beauty and orderliness of nature (e.g. the reliability of the laws of science, so predictable that we can argue ahead from them – that's how the planet Pluto was discovered); it is so complex and wonderful (and so are you) that it could not have happened by chance. It took a Designer and a Creator to make you.

15 The four bases of prayer mentioned earlier are in fact the bases of our duty to God as his children. This duty is collectively called worship, and we owe him worship both private and public – because although you are his own unique and special child, you are a social creature; you need to relate to others, and you are affected by the doings of others (you are not an island).

We mentioned prayer earlier as something private; now we look at public worship. Man has always felt the need to acknowledge a supreme being, and apart from saying and singing in public, there has always been the notion of offering sacrifice. This means to "make holy", and this is done by setting aside something precious to give to God (in whatever way he is understood – even as a black stone in the middle of a village on which humans might be slaughtered). At the most basic level, if something or somebody is sacrificed (given to God) it is killed, and then often burned, to show that once given to God it cannot be taken back for our own use.

We have the Sacrifice of the Mass, which is the continued offering to God of the Sacrifice of Jesus on the Cross, the sacrifice which made up to God for all the sins of humankind; and the Resurrection of Jesus is the sign above all others that he is divine, and also that his sacrifice was accepted by his eternal Father. More about the Mass later (see 22-25).

16 Another important digression: in the beginning there was God, by himself, and in need of no one else. When you are full of happiness and delight, you often like to have someone to share your joy. God did not need to share his goodness and his happiness, but he still chose to do so, and first he created the angels for this. They are pure spirits; they do not have or need bodies, and their minds and wills are far more powerful than ours.

As you know, you are happiest with somebody who you love because they love you. The angels would be happy with God if they loved him, so he gave them some sort of test, a chance to use their free will to choose and show whether they loved him, or preferred themselves (whether they would accept his will or preferred their own). We don't know what that test was, but we do know that some angels accepted and some refused.

Those who by God's grace accepted, merited by their acceptance to see him face to face (in heaven and wherever else he requires them to work: especially he appoints to each of us a guardian to be with us throughout our lives – but sadly many people are unaware of this great privilege, and those who were taught about it when young tend to forget about it later).

The chief of the angels who obeyed God is Michael the archangel, and we know of two others of his rank: Gabriel who was sent to tell Mary that she was to be the Mother of God, and Raphael the healer. The angel who comforted Jesus in his dreadful agony in Gethsemane is not known by name, but would have been one of the great ones.

The angels who rebelled brought hell into existence by their rebellion, and were cast into it. They are called devils or demons. The chief of the angels who rebelled against God is Satan – originally known as Lucifer, the light-bearer – the source of all our temptation and ultimately of all that is evil. Satan and his rebel angels are supremely jealous of God's earthly children, and they long to destroy God's plan for us by winning us over to their side against God. This they do by trying to persuade us to sin. But temptation is not sin: we sin only when we deliberately make a decision of our will which results in thoughts, words, deeds or omissions which we know to be wrong.

17 We don't know when he created the universe, or how long passed before our planet became habitable by man. We don't believe that he created the world in six days of twenty-four hour periods such we are used to now, but we must always remember that the first books of the Bible were compiled at a time when few people knew how to read or write, and all necessary truths were passed on from generation to generation by word of mouth. The easiest way to remember these was to have them in story form. Nevertheless, those early chapters of the book of Genesis contain as much of God's divine revelation as he saw fit to give at that time: that he created all things, that he created our first parents (whom we know as Adam and Eve), that he gave them a command (to give them the chance to use their free will to prove that they loved him by obeying him), that in fact they disobeyed him, that they were consequently punished by losing his divine life from their souls, and by having to lose their natural life at last by death – and that God promised that a Redeemer would come at last.

18 There need be no difficulty about evolution, so long as we remember that man as a human is different from the animals

(he is a reasoning animal), and his reasoning power cannot have evolved. An animal cannot be (or become) capable of abstract thought – it cannot (and could never) grasp truth, beauty, goodness, evil in the abstract: you can train it to act in certain ways and to avoid other sorts of behaviour, but it will act by instinct and association of ideas; if a dog worries sheep, you don't take the dog to court, because you know that the dog is not morally responsible. In addition, the human is of an entirely higher order because he has an immortal soul, destined by God to be with him for eternity.

19 For our first parents to disobey God was in a way much less excusable than for us, since their lower appetites were under control (we have to train ours and it's sometimes difficult): Satan had to attack the citadel of their minds, by trying to convince them that God was holding out on them, even deceiving them.

After that, God was under no obligation to restore them from their disgrace, but his love and pity are so great that he chose to make it possible for us humans to regain his friendship.

The angels got no second chance: their sin was far greater, since they would have seen God and his goodness so much more clearly than Adam and Eve did, and they were not tempted from outside, either; also, God would have known that any grace of repentance offered would be rejected, so great was their pride and hatred of him.

20 We measure a wrong partly by the thing done, but we also take into account the kind of person wronged (it's even worse to kill a friend than a stranger). But God is our Creator and loving Father, and man simply wasn't good enough to put right by himself the damage done to his precious relationship with God by his rebellion against him.

So he sent his Son Jesus to become a man and thus represent mankind in his atoning (or making good) to God for man's rebellion. Notice that this rebellion does not consist merely of the first disobedience of Adam and Eve (our original sin): it also includes all the sins actually committed by every person – and because Jesus loves his Father (and ours) without limit, he was willing to carry out his Father's plan. Remember that Jesus has always existed as the Second Person of the Blessed Trinity (Father, Son and Holy Spirit) – and that God knew from the first that man would sin, and that he would send his Son to redeem him. (Why create someone he knew would rebel? Why send his Son to redeem us at such cost? This is the mystery of his love which we can't fathom in this life – nor shall we completely in the next either. Still, we can say that we have the strongest motive for returning his love now that we know what he has done in creating each of us, and what he endured for each of us).

In everything that God does, all three Persons of the Trinity act together as one. Thus God died for us on Calvary, but only because Jesus took to himself a human nature in which he could die.

21 This brings us to the purposes of Jesus's time on earth. He came in order to die for us and to rise again, so as to make good to his Father and ours for the sins of mankind and to show that his Father had accepted the sacrifice he made of himself on our behalf. He came also to teach us by his word and example, so that we could, with his help, acquire our intended status as the adopted children of his Father (by being baptised), and become more and more like him by becoming more and more holy, by pleasing him in all that we think, say and do. In his life, and especially in his suffering and death on the cross, he offered himself as a victim of sacrifice on behalf of each single one of us.

His chief commands (to love God above all things, and to love each other as he himself has loved us) are difficult to keep: but he backed up his teachings by his miracles – they show that he is God and thus has the right to command us, but his miracles, and above all his death and resurrection, also show his immense love for us, and so he prompts us to love him in return, and to show our love by trying to live according to his commands. He will always help us in our efforts to do this, but he will never try to force our free will: if he did, we should become machines and no longer able freely to show him any love. Equally, though he will strengthen us against temptation if we ask his help, he will never override anyone's intention to use his free will wrongly. That accounts for all the evil that man commits.

22 The help that he gives us (his grace, his free gift always available for us) comes to us mainly in three ways: through the Mass, the Sacraments and prayer. In our Mass we share in his offering of himself on the cross for our sins. This he did once and for all centuries ago, but in the Mass he continues to offer himself to the Father through the hands of the priest. In his suffering and dying he showed unlimited love and praise for his Father, thanks for his goodness to us his children, sorrow for his children's sins and pleading for all our needs – the four bases of prayer and of sacrifice.

This love and praise, this thanks, sorrow and pleading of his he has left us in the Mass, and we go on offering it to the Father through the centuries at his command ("Do this in memory of me", he said at the Last Supper, which was the first Mass). By our Baptism into Christ we become members of his family (which we call his Mystical Body), and so have the right to share in the offering of the Mass which is the public worship we owe him. In the Mass we unite our own love and praise, our thanks, sorrow and pleading, with that of Jesus on the cross – and it is this that gives value to our offering.

Additionally, of course, we should always try to unite the suffering in our lives with the suffering of Jesus on the cross. It is not always easy to think of this at times of great pain, but we should always expressly include this in our offering of ourselves each time we attend Mass. Then our offering and union with Jesus will still hold good when our own cross is hard to bear.

23 That is why we are told to "go to Mass" every week – it is far better to understand ourselves as being told to "assist in the offering of the Mass" every week: that can give us a strong motive for being there (partly for our own benefit, and very much for the needs of others all over the world, needs often far greater than our own). It is true that we don't offer the Mass in precisely the same way that the priest does (he has to remember always, poor mere man that he is, that he stands in the person of Christ in that offering – so please keep priests in your prayers) – but our offering is none the less real, and powerful because of its union with the offering of Christ himself. St Peter calls us "a chosen people, a royal priesthood" (1 Peter 2, 9):

every Sunday (or Saturday evening) and on certain other great days in the year (the Holydays of Obligation), we have the duty and privilege of taking part in that great act of public worship for the sake of every one of God's children – primarily to give supreme honour and glory (worship) to God, for the conversion of sinners, and to make the Church holy.

24 For this purpose, think of yourself as the centre of several concentric circles: you offer your Mass for your own self, but at the same time you are sharing in the public offering of this sacrifice of Jesus Christ with very many others (because he offered himself for all): first for your family and friends and all their needs: then for people brought to your attention in the Mass, notably the members of the parish or other group you are with, then for other special people (especially all sinners, those suffering injustice or oppression, the hungry, the grieving – the list is endless). Before the Mass begins, decide who it is that you are going to offer your Mass for specially.

Besides, always remember that you are a cell in the Mystical Body of Christ (see 22 above) with the duty of contributing to its health (its holiness) – also, if you fall into sin, the health (the holiness) of the whole Body suffers.

25 Because you will have spent your effort in the Mass for the needs of others, Jesus is not going to be outdone in generosity. You may be sure that he will give you all kinds of help as and when you most need it, to help you to see what you must do to love him better, and to show this in the way you treat others (because they also are his children).

26 Another of the ways in which he gives you his grace (and thus more of his divine life in your soul) is through the Sacraments; those designed for the development of your day-to-day relationship with him are Holy Communion and the Sacrament of Reconciliation. The third way is prayer (see below, 35-60).

Baptism brought you into his family, and Confirmation gives you the strength to deepen your commitment to him and to his work, but in Holy Communion he gives you life and strength (read what Jesus says in chapter 6 of St John's Gospel, verses 51 to 69, and especially 55 to 57) – and in the Sacrament of Reconciliation (Confession) he gives you comfort and consolation. We need to meet him regularly in both these Sacraments if we are to keep our love for him growing and deepening; our love grows stronger because he is the food and strength of our soul, and especially our mind and our will.

27 The worst thing possible that can happen is for us to fall into mortal sin. It is called "mortal" because it literally kills God's life in the soul. As a result we are spiritually dead, and it is no longer possible for us to reach heaven, for which God created us. Satan has won us to his side, and if we die in that state we shall join him in hell – not because God has sent us there, but because we have chosen to reject God's love and thus could not be happy with him anyway. (Remember that for a sin to be mortal, it must be gravely wrong, we must know that it is gravely wrong, and there must be full consent to it in our will).

Generally speaking, if somebody has been trying steadily to please God by protecting the spiritual life he has given us (by using his means of grace, namely assisting in the offering of the Mass, receiving the Sacraments, regular prayer) it is most unlikely that such a person will fall into mortal sin.

It is when we begin to be careless about our spiritual lives, when we take less and less notice of our minor faults, that our love for Jesus gradually cools and our spiritual danger becomes greater. Satan is always on the lookout.

28 We should never be afraid to confess any sin, no matter how grave, no matter how ashamed we may feel. Remember that Jesus will always welcome us back with joy when we come to him and tell him we are truly sorry. Even if we fear that temptation will be too much for us and that we shall fall again, what he is looking for is that we are sorry *now*. Remember that the priest is himself a sinner (and he must never dare to forget it), and that he has the special power and duty (and privilege) laid upon him by Jesus to give you with certainty Jesus's own forgiveness, strength and consolation, so that you can be absolutely sure that you have left your burden behind you with Jesus after receiving his grace and forgiveness in this

Sacrament. The graces that Jesus gives the priest include being able to rejoice with him (and with you) at your courage in co-operating with the grace of Jesus, to whom you have come for forgiveness. Any priest will tell you that his moments of greatest joy have been the times when he has been present when God's grace has reconciled someone to his Creator.

29 Never forget that when God forgives us he still requires us to do penance in this life or the next. If it seems somehow unfair that there should be a form of punishment after forgiveness, remember that Our Lord himself alone has already borne the full weight of his Father's just punishment for the sins of man, but that he still wishes us to recognise the enormity of rebelling against his loving Father, and there can be nothing unjust about that.

Imagine that a small boy has broken a window with his ball (after being warned to be careful), and that he has been told that the ball will be confiscated for a month, that he will see no television during that time, that he is to dry the dishes after every meal for a month, and that his pocket-money will be stopped until the new glass is paid for.

Of course he is sorry, and says so in no uncertain terms. So his father relents and lets him off the punishments, except that the boy still has to pay for the new glass. That may be seen as something like our own situation – though Our Lord may accept very great sorrow in place of penance.

30 We say the penance given us by the priest in Confession, of course, but we are not to presume that this will be all the penance Our Lord requires of us, and we should add to it various acts of self-denial in our daily life, as well as trying willingly to accept the trials and sufferings that he sends or allows to come to us. This is sometimes hard, but remember that his grace is always enough for us (see what he said to St Paul in 2 Corinthians 12, 9).

31 Provided there is nothing serious on our conscience between us and Jesus, we should try to receive him in Holy Communion whenever we go to Mass (this will complete our sharing in the offering of the Sacrifice) – and it is wise to receive

his special help in the Sacrament of Reconciliation in any case every four to six weeks (otherwise our daily faults begin to happen more often and we notice them less), or more often if we are enduring any strong temptations. Not only does Jesus forgive our sins in this Sacrament (and restore the life of our soul and thus our union with him if it has been destroyed by mortal sin), he also heals the effects of venial sin and makes our conscience more sensitive to right and wrong. He also strengthens and consoles us, and sharpens our longing to receive him again in Holy Communion. If ever we suspect that our receiving him in Holy Communion is in any danger at all of becoming a matter of mere routine, the first thing to do is to ask ourselves how long it is since we received his special graces in the Sacrament of Reconciliation (in other words, how long since we went to Confession).

32 How does Jesus give you more of his divine life in Holy Communion? We say that in Holy Communion he feeds our souls, and we need to realise the meaning of this in ever greater depth. Read carefully what he says in the Gospel of St John, chapter 6, versus 53-57; think slowly about what he says and ask him to help you to understand it more and more clearly. You will see that receiving him in Holy Communion is absolutely essential for the development in ourselves of the share in his life which we received in Baptism. For this life cannot be developed without his grace, and he gives us his own very self as the special means for this.

33 When he enters a soul that welcomes him, he feeds it with his love, his light and his strength and thus draws it more closely to himself. The hold of self within the soul is weakened – self is your greatest enemy and Satan's ally within you. He comes with gifts, the gifts especially of his Holy Spirit, which enable your mind to see more clearly that he is your Way, your Truth and your Life; they also give strength to *your* will to live out your daily life according to *his* will.

34 A most important time of adoration, love and thanks is immediately after you have received Jesus in Holy Communion. He is actually there within you as your guest, and in a sense you have him there all to yourself. Use this time well, and be

prepared to stay behind in church for this purpose after Mass is over: after all, it is at that time that it is easiest to know his closeness to you (even if you do not actually feel him to be close, he is in fact right there in the most special way).

35 This leads directly into the third main way in which God gives us his grace: when we pray. But just what is praying? It is sometimes called "talking to God", but it is much better thought of as "talking *with* God", or just being aware of his presence and responding in love.

Your feelings (emotions, if you like) have an important part here, though they are often not mentioned in connection with praying. As noted earlier, each of us longs to love and to be loved. It would be hard to say which is the more important. But our feelings can sometimes help us very much in our reaching out in love, and in our longing for love. One day a crippled teenager was watching another boy carrying his little brother on his back, and the teenager said "I wish I could be a brother like that". (Think about it – he didn't say "I wish I could have a brother like that").

36 We long to have someone special in our lives that we can always rely on, always turn to – someone whose company we can always be happy in. At first our parents fill that role, but we grow out of that sort of relationship with them. We find something of the kind in other people, close friends made in our teens (and often kept for life), and looking for the right girl or boy has something of this in it too.

37 But our seeking has a spiritual element as well – instinctively we reach out for someone more reliable, that we can depend on absolutely no matter what. In fact, as St Augustine said, God has made us for himself, and our hearts are restless till they find rest in him. At your age praying is a reaching out, almost into a sort of dark, hoping that there is someone there, even longing for there to be. You may feel that you have grown out of your simple childhood prayers; though they will always have their importance, you want to reach out beyond those ideas – but you don't know what to say.

38 That is where your prayer begins to grow. If you are willing to ask Our Lord, and keep on asking him in all sincerity, you can be certain that he will not desert you. He may reward you by allowing you to feel his presence, but you must not expect to feel it; it is enough for you to know that he is there. And you must not worry if you do not *feel* that you love God: it is most important to remember that love is mainly a matter of the will, rather than of the emotions.

If you don't feel like praying, just go on praying anyway (and don't feel guilty about not feeling like praying – it's a common experience). Jesus will value your effort all the more, because it shows your love for him all the more clearly.

39 Do you feel that prayer is sometimes very one-sided? Do you wonder whether it's worth going on if nothing seems to happen as a result? Was it worth sharing your inmost thoughts, your hopes, fears and ideals with someone who perhaps wasn't listening? Remember that God created you by his own special choice, and that he will always listen (because he loves you, if for no other reason). And he will always reply – but not in words: most usually by ideas, and sometimes you will even see that these ideas must have come at least partly from him.

You tell him that you love him, you thank him, you tell him that you are sorry for all kinds of things (and he knows you mean it) – but what about the times when you ask him for things, really important things really urgently needed by other people, and nothing seems to result?

40 There is *always* an answer – but sometimes the answer will be "not yet", or "not in the way you want or may expect", or sometimes even simply "no": he always knows what is best for you, and for those you pray for. And sometimes that is very hard indeed to accept. (But see the note about the tapestry below, in 48).

41 We may grow only slowly in our union with Jesus: it takes time, and we need to work at it, remembering that all the growth comes from his drawing us closer to himself. The only obstacle to this is your own selfish desires. You must ask him to

help you to overcome them, and then really work at them under his grace.

42 Above all, you *must* find proper time every morning and evening for being with him in prayer. Because we are mostly creatures of routine, it will probably be best for you to settle on fixed times each day, to be sure of enough time to give him. If you really do wish to become more like him, you *must* spend as much time as you can with him. You may need to rethink your priorities about this quite seriously. To start with, try to give him at least five minutes in the morning and ten minutes in the evening. Ask him to help you to be strict with yourself, and to aim to give him longer – there will probably be more time in the evening if you make up your mind to it. Even though it may often be convenient to do your spiritual reading in the evening, and to go straight into your prayer from it, the time spent reading should not count towards the time you spend with him! However, don't feel that you must always read before you pray (see below) – just be sure to give him enough time.

43 Try to choose a time and place of silence, so that you can be sure of starting the day under his protection, and looking forward to the peace of being with him after the stress of the day. Be alone, and reasonably comfortable (pray on your knees, but only for as long as you comfortably can).

Clear your mind by asking for his help, and either do a little bit of reading, or close your eyes and put yourself into a mental picture of the sort mentioned later on. Then you can go on thinking of him in connection with the scene in which you have placed yourself, and let your heart (your will) reach out to him in love, adoration, thanks, sorrow, or asking (see 53 below). Reading is only reading, and the thinking is only meditation – it is the raising of your mind and heart to him that is prayer. You may sometimes find that reading and thinking will bring you to a dead stop. Don't get tense about it – concentrate on relaxing, and wait. Don't forget that praying must include listening too. Just try to stay with him and be at peace.

44 Quite often you will not want to use words when you pray. This can be for a number of reasons, and will be especially true

at times when you have strong feelings (of happiness, joy, delight, love, grief, shock, anger, doubt and so on). At those times don't try to use words – just be with him in your heart, and share your feelings with him. If your feelings involve other people, bring them into your prayer; have them there in a mental picture with Jesus (see next paragraph). It is particularly helpful to have near you a crucifix or a picture of Jesus, or of Our Lady. If you get used to its being in the same place, so that you don't notice it any more, move it to a different place, so that you will be aware of it when you wake, and before you go to bed.

45 This is a good time to think about where your imagination comes in, for it is much easier to be with someone in your heart and share your feelings with them if you can have a picture of them in your mind. You have seen pictures of Jesus many times, and it is often not too hard to imagine yourself sitting talking with him, or kneeling beside him – or even simply holding his hand in the dark in times of great sadness. Remember that he understands your joys and your tears better than anyone else can – this is (of course) because he is God, but also because he is still human too, and he has suffered more and worse than we have, even in our hardest times. The scenes listed below will often help you (see 47).

46 There will be times when your imagination is no help at all, either because you have not tried to settle yourself properly to pray, or because Jesus does not allow you the consolation of being aware that he is with you.

If you have not settled yourself properly to pray, your imagination will run wild and you will be distracted. Even when you have tried to put yourself in the presence of Jesus before beginning to pray, your imagination may still interfere and carry your thoughts away with it. When this happens, keep trying to get back to Jesus again. Distractions come to everyone, but they do not spoil our prayer if we turn them away from us. If you feel exhausted at the end of prayer-time spent almost entirely in trying to be rid of distractions, do not suppose that your prayer has been worthless – in fact it has all been a generous act of love.

Do not feel upset (that is what Satan is aiming at) – just go on praying peacefully in God's presence and regardless of the distractions.

47 There are many "set pieces" which you can use for your mental picture if at any time you may find them attractive; many of the Gospel scenes, for instance:

a) kneeling with the shepherds in the stable after Jesus is born, adoring him and loving him (Luke 2. 6-19);

b) watching old Simeon as he holds the Babe in his arms, listening to what he says to Mary, and imagining her mixture of anxiety, trust and love (Luke 2. 22-35);

c) being present at the wedding at Cana, hearing the conversation between Jesus and his mother, and seeing what happened then (John 2. 1-12);

d) sitting with his disciples and listening to him teaching them during the Sermon on the Mount (Matthew 5.1 to 7.28 – take this in small sections);

e) watching him perform some of his miracles (always motivated by love and pity for somebody else – he did no miracles for his own benefit) (e.g. Matthew 8.1 to 9.37 – again take this in small sections);

f) being present during his feeding of the five thousand and his promise of giving himself to us in Holy Communion (John 6. 1-69, especially 1-15 and 51-69);

g) being on the holy mountain with Peter, James and John and with them seeing and hearing what happened (Matthew 17. 1-8);

h) being with them all at the Last Supper (John 13. 1-30 – small sections again);

i) being with the eleven and listening to his teaching and the conversation that followed the Last Supper (John 13.31 to 16.33 – take this in very small bits);

j) hearing his prayer before they left the upper room (John 17. 1-26);

k) following him very slowly through his Passion: you will find this sequence useful;

1) go into the Garden of Gethsemane with Peter, James and John; he is a little ahead of you. Mark tells you what happens (14. 32-52);

2) stay with Mark, for he is telling Peter's story (14.53 to 15.47);

3) then turn to John (who was there at the foot of the cross) and hear what Jesus says to him and to his mother (19. 25-30);

4) John goes on to tell the remaining events of that day (19. 31-42);

After 1) above, you may prefer to vary the sequence by picturing carefully each of the fourteen Stations of the Cross. In either case, go very slowly, and do not try to take on more than you can stand. Keep his special love for you always in mind.

l) go to the tomb with the women very early on the Sunday morning, and follow the events as John records them (20. 1-10, then 11-18);

m) set out for Emmaus with Cleopas and his friend, and read Luke's account of what happened (24. 13-42);

n) join the disciples in the upper room for Jesus appearing to them that same evening – and again a week later when Thomas was there too (John 20. 19-29).

You can supplement all these, or use a different approach, by taking the fifteen different events noted in the mysteries of the Rosary and using them as the basis for your prayer.

48 Sometimes (and especially at times of distress) think of God's tapestry of creation. A tapestry is a woven picture, consisting of a pattern of very many threads. The top of the tapestry is its beginning, at the start of creation, and the picture goes on lengthening as the centuries pass, and now it has reached the present year, month, date, hour, minute, second.

The complete picture exists in God's mind, but only he can see the whole picture; we are so close to it – we are inside it in fact, because we are ourselves part of it – that we can't see why some threads are long and others short, why some are dark and others bright, some are weak and others strong.

God makes his picture the way he does because he loves each single living thread, and knows how each will best fit in with his full and complete plan of love given and returned.

49 When life runs smoothly it is easy to tell God that you love him (and to mean it sincerely), and he values your love. But if in hard times you can tell him that you want to love him as much as ever in spite of everything, he knows how much that is costing you to say and to mean, and he values your love even more for that reason.

50 You will see from the above that your prayer needs to be fed (you need to have something to pray about, or at least to start you off), and that some working knowledge of the life of Jesus is essential. Try to acquire this gradually: never set yourself a fixed amount to be read every day or every week. Read very slowly, allowing your imagination time to put before you the pictures you need. Stop when any scene appeals to you particularly strongly, or when something Jesus says seems especially important (he will help you with this if you ask him before the start).

51 But remember that all this reading is never more than a starting-point; it is only a spring-board for your prayer. Its purpose is to help you to want to love him better, more deeply. That must always be the bedrock – the longing to deepen your relationship with him, and it is a relationship of love.

52 It goes without saying that sin will always damage prayer because it will cool the warmth of your love for Jesus to a greater or lesser extent – and truly mortal sin will certainly kill it. Yet if your efforts to love have been strong and sincere, Jesus will always hear when you tell him of your grief and be willing to take you back, and to comfort you (i.e. give you consolation and strength). As you saw earlier, the Sacrament of Reconciliation is the wonderful means which he has left us for this. In the

case of truly mortal sin, it is an absolute essential, of course –
even if it is not immediately possible for us to go to Confession,
our being sorry for mortal sin must include the intention of
meeting Jesus in this Sacrament as soon as we can manage it.

53 What should you pray about? See 12 above: adore him,
love him, praise him, thank him, tell him you are sorry for sin
because you love him (especially your own sins but also those of
others – but be careful not to judge them in doing this: and
remember that though we must hate sin, we may never hate the
sinner). Pray for others, pray for yourself – the graces they need,
the graces you need, especially the help you need to become
more and more like Jesus (see details below).

a) In particular, ask him to increase your faith, your trust
   and your love, and to deepen your knowledge and
   understanding of the Faith, and to strengthen your
   courage and patience (both to accept his will for you in
   your daily life, and in standing up for your beliefs). Ask
   him to be with you in times of temptation, and to help you
   to persevere in prayer. Ask him to help you to know your
   sins and your weaknesses and to acknowledge them
   humbly and without fear.

b) Pray to your guardian angel every morning and every
   night. God has appointed him to be with you throughout
   your life. Remember that he is with you every minute of
   every day and every night: learn to love him, and to thank
   him for looking after you and guiding you. It is so easy to
   forget him otherwise, and that would be lack of gratitude
   to him, and of course to God for giving him to you for your
   very own.

c) Don't forget to pray to your patron saints – especially to
   the one whose name you chose for your Confirmation. Try
   to find out more about your saints, so as to follow their
   example.

d) Pray also for those closest to you (family; friends;
   enemies). Pray for those who you know need your help
   (those who have asked you to pray for them; the sick and
   the dying, and those who care for them; sinners;

agnostics; atheists). Pray for world leaders, that they may allow themselves to be guided by God's grace.

e) Remember the Holy Souls especially: they have a particular claim on your love.

f) Pray for the needs of the Church (of which you are a member) – pray for your own parish, especially your priests; pray for the Holy Father and for the bishops of the world (they all need God's guidance); ask God for more vocations to the priesthood and to the religious life (monasteries and convents are the power-houses of the Church); ask God to help young people to be more generous in heeding his call and acting upon it. Pray for teachers, especially that they may remember the great responsibility God has laid on them.

g) Remember how much you have to thank God for: this will not be hard if you count your blessings (especially things you perhaps take for granted, such as your talents and your health) and think of others less fortunate.

54 You need not include each of the four forms of prayer every time, but at least be sure to include your prayer of love and adoration every day, especially asking him for the grace to love him for his own sake rather than for any hope of reward. He will always give you the grace for this (but at the time and in the measure that he knows is best – and again remember that you must not expect to *feel* his presence or his love: it is enough to know that he is there).

55 Then in return for his grace you will give him the selfless love that he longs for: it is his own love that you are returning, for you are letting him produce a clearer and clearer reflection of himself in your soul as he takes over more and more from self (your greatest enemy and Satan's best ally, remember).

56 For your soul is rather like the sort of mirror that was used in Our Lord's time on earth: it was a metal plate, of bronze or some other metal, and (like your soul) could only give as clear a reflection as was brought about by the constant smoothing away of dents and distortions and the polishing away of scratches and blemishes. Only Jesus can produce this clear

reflection of himself within you, and he will do it only if you ask him for the great favour of this grace, and only if you allow him to bring it about in his own good time by putting yourself completely in his hands (and leaving yourself there) – see 62 below.

As also noted below (61), be patient: this process of our coming to reflect Jesus in our souls is gradual, and we do not realise that we are hindering Jesus every time we allow self to rule our daily lives.

57 Remember the value of our set prayers, especially those handed down to us through the centuries: of course particularly Our Lord's own prayer, and the Hail Mary and the Glory Be. These are especially useful in praying for other people. Then the Apostles' Creed or the long Creed used at Mass are valuable for your own prayer, because they are so powerful an expression of your adoration and love of God, and because they contain so many of the treasures of your faith. You can turn those great jewels over in your mind as you say these prayers. Never rush these prayers, in fact sometimes use them as spring-boards for deeper prayer: take a single statement or petition and think about what it means (for instance, the simple words "Our Father" – why 'our', why 'Father'?), and then go on to talk with God using the ideas that these words give you. Never feel that you must "get through" any fixed amount of a prayer at these times: stay with a few words for as long as they help you to keep your mind and heart on God.

58 Remember what he teaches us to say in the Lord's Prayer about forgiving one another: we cannot hope for his forgiveness unless we have ourselves already forgiven everyone who has wronged us in any way. It is true that forgiving and forgetting are not the same (forgiving is an act of your will, but forgetting is a matter of your memory), but if we find it hard to forgive, we must ask God for the grace we need to make us able to forgive – and at the same time ask for his grace to heal our memory too. Your goodwill towards the person you have forgiven (which results from God's grace) will itself begin the healing process.

59 Our night prayers should include a short examination of our conscience, during which we check through the day and tell Jesus that we are sorry for times when we have failed to live up to what he wants of us, and it is a good time to consider what we can do by way of penance.

This may include prayer (especially visiting Jesus in the Blessed Sacrament – a generous sacrifice of your time for his sake), fasting (giving up any pleasure at your own choice), and almsgiving (not necessarily money, but also giving up some of your time to do things for other people, or again spiritual almsgiving in the way of penance or reparation for the sins of others).

60 Because the graces of Holy Communion and the Sacrament of Reconciliation all strengthen our union with Jesus, it follows that our prayer-life will gain every time we receive them – and the more devoutly we receive his graces, the more our prayer-life will deepen as a result (but remember that this does *not* mean that we shall necessarily find praying easier).

61 Finally, be patient with yourself, and above all be patient with Jesus. You will long to feel his nearness (especially during hard times), but *you must always remember* that he will draw you to himself in his own way, in his own time, and that he knows your longings better than you do yourself.

Refer all your uncertainties, your hopes and fears to him. Ask him to help with all your decisions. It will take time to develop this habit and at times it will be difficult, for it means in fact that you are gradually surrendering yourself completely into his hands, and thus going against the grain of your natural pride. But this is the only way to get out of his path while he trains you to be more and more like him – more Christlike, more and more a Christian.

62 It is the greatest possible sign of your love for him if you are willing to put yourself entirely into his hands – not just in the matter of your prayer and union, but in every single moment of every single day of your life. After all, there can be no safer place to be. Once you are willing to make such an act of

surrender, he will never let you fall. But you must expect Satan to attack you fiercely with his temptations, especially pride – he will try many times and in many ways to persuade you that you are the only one that matters.

63 To keep up your strength, try to attend Mass often, receive the Sacraments with great love and regularly, and be sure to pray every day. Especially remember that Jesus's Mother Mary is there to protect you. She is the Queen of the angels, and her power over Satan is very great. Remember to pray regularly to your guardian angel too (see 53b above): he is always in touch with her.

64 Above all, *do not* try to rely on yourself alone: the forces of evil are very strong, and a disgraced angel is far more powerful in the natural order than a mere human. If you become proud you will lose sight of that – and that is how he will try to entice you to forget that the only safe place for you to be is in the hands of God. In times of temptation you may not feel God's presence (even though he is with you), and that is the time especially to turn to Mary for her help and protection.

65 When Satan tries to discourage you, at those times Mary will always be your strong shield by reason of the graces that she will obtain for you. She sees your needs and has a mother's love for you.

This prayer will always help you; say it regularly and you will soon learn it:

> Remember, O most loving Virgin Mary,
> that it is a thing unheard of
> that anyone ever had recourse to your protection,
> implored your help,
> or sought your intercession
> and was left forsaken.
> Filled, therefore, with confidence in your goodness,
> I fly to you, O Mother, Virgin of virgins;
> to you I come,
> before you I stand,
> a sorrowful sinner.

Despise not my poor words,
O Mother of the Word of God,
but graciously hear and grant my prayer.   Amen.

Another that you should use regularly (and so come to know by heart):

Hail, holy Queen, mother of mercy.
Hail, our life, our sweetness and our hope.
To thee do we cry, poor banished children of Eve.
To thee do we send up our sighs,
    mourning and weeping in this vale of tears.
Turn then, most gracious advocate,
    thine eyes of mercy towards us,
and after this, our exile, show unto us
    the blessed fruit of thy womb, Jesus.
O clement, O loving, O sweet Virgin Mary.

And you may like to add:

Pray for us, O holy Mother of God.
That we may be made worthy of the promises of Christ.

Then any one of the following:

Lord Jesus Christ, you chose the Virgin Mary to be your mother,
    a worthy home in which to dwell.
By her prayers keep us from danger
and bring us to the joy of heaven.
    where you live and reign with the Father and the Holy Spirit,
    one God, for ever and ever.   Amen.

Lord God, give to your people the joy
of continual health in mind and body.
With the prayers of the Virgin Mary to help us,
guide us through the sorrows of this life
to eternal happiness in the life to come.
We make our prayer through Christ our Lord.   Amen.

Lord, take away the sins of your people.
May the prayers of Mary the mother of your Son help us,
for alone and unaided we cannot hope to please you.
We ask this through Christ our Lord.   Amen.

God of mercy, give us strength.
May we who honour the blessed Mother of God
rise above our sins and failings with the help of her prayers.
Through Christ our Lord.   Amen.

Lord, may the prayers of the Virgin Mary
bring us protection from danger and freedom from sin,
so that we may come to the joy of your peace.
We ask this through Christ our Lord.   Amen.